Best Traditional Irish Recipes for St. Patrick's Day

About the Author

Laura Sommers is **The Recipe Lady!**

She is the #1 Best Selling Author of over 80 recipe books.

She is a loving wife and mother who lives on a small farm in Baltimore County, Maryland and has a passion for all things domestic especially when it comes to saving money. She has a profitable eBay business and is a couponing addict, avid blogger and YouTuber.

Follow her tips and tricks to learn how to make delicious meals on a budget, save money or to learn the latest life hack!

Visit her blog for even more great recipes and to learn which books are **FREE** for download each week:

http://the-recipe-lady.blogspot.com/

Visit her Amazon Author Page to see her latest books:

amazon.com/author/laurasommers

© Copyright 2016. Laura Sommers.
All rights reserved.
No part of this book may be reproduced in any form or by any electronic or mechanical means without written permission of the author. All text, illustrations and design are the exclusive property of
Laura Sommers

Dedicated to my daughter, Fiona.

My little Irish Princess.

About the Author ii

Introduction 1

St. Patrick's Day Corned Beef and Cabbage 2

Irish Soda Bread 3

Irish Champ 4

Paddy's Colcannon 5

Emerald Isle Shepherd's Pie 6

Irish Lamb Stew 7

Potato Cakes 8

Emerald Isle Beef in Guinness 9

Gooseberry Crumble 10

Dublin Coddle 11

Potato Casserole 12

Fried Cabbage and Bacon 13

Potato Soup 14

Irish Boxty 15

Guinness Mustard 16

Dublin Iced Coffee 17

Dublin Lawyer 18

Irish Cabbage Rolls 19

Colcannon Bake 20

Irish Liver and Onions 21

Irish Heritage Cabbage 22

Irish Corn O'Brien 23

Irish Scalloped Potatoes 24

Irish Quick Hoppin' John	25
Irish Soda Farls	26
Cornbread and Beef Skillet Pie	27
Sweet Potato Corned Beef Hash	28
Irish Nachos	29
Green Silver Dollar Pancakes	31
Chocolate Stout Crepes with Irish Cream Whip	32
Irish Wheaten Bread	34
Guinness Beef Stew	35
Irish Potato Bread	36
Irish Veda Bread	37
Irish Beer Bread	38
Irish Pork Chops with Cabbage and Apples	39
Irish Breakfast Fry Up	40
Irish Fish and Chips	41
Irish Cheese and Bacon Potatoes	42
Irish Leprechaun Chow Snack Mix	43
Irish Cornish Pastie	44
Irish Purple Cabbage & Pecan Salad	45
Irish Black Pudding	46
Irish Crisp Sandwich	47
Irish Soda Bread Pudding	48
Irish Chicken and Dumplings	49
Irish Chicken and Leek Pie	50
Irish Root Soup	51
Irish Soda Bread Cookies	52
Irish Cream Sugar Cookies	53

Irish Shamrock Cookies	54
Irish Flag Cookies	55
Irish Oatmeal Cookies	56
Highland Toffee	57
Irish Peanut Butter Potato Candy	58
Irish Potatoes	59
Irish Cream Truffles	60
Bailey's Irish Cream Brownies	61
Irish Cream Truffle Fudge	62
Irish Cream Bundt Cake	63
Irish Ginger Snaps	64
Avocado Irish Cream Fudge	65
Irish Cream Chocolate Cheesecake	66
Irish Bannock	67
Irish Bananas	68
Irish Barmbrack	69
Irish Apple Pie	70
Irish Beef and Guinness Pies	72
Lucky Charms Cookies	74
Lucky Charms Eclairs	75
Irish Earl Grey Tea Cookies	77
Irish Thin-Mint Grasshopper Pie	78
Fried Irish Cabbage with Bacon	79
Irish Lucky Charms Cheesecakes	80
Irish Blueberry Scones	81
Irish Lemon Pudding	82
Irish Beef Beer Stew	83

Irish Tea Cake	84
Irish Whiskey and Beer Cupcakes	85
Irish Stout and Chocolate Cheesecake	87
Irish Cheese Soup	89
Bangers and Mash	90
Irish Cheese Dip	91
Irish Toast	92
Irish Brown Bread	93
Irish Stuffed Baked Potato	94
About the Author	95
Other books in This Series	96

Introduction

Whether it's St. Patrick's Day or not, everyone has a little luck o' the Irish in them. Now you can create all your favorite traditional Irish favorites from home baked bread to comforting soups. The Irish kitchen is a warm welcoming place. This cookbook contains all the traditional recipes as well as some Irish inspired creations. With simple step-by-step instructions, creating these delicious meals couldn't be easier.

St. Patrick's Day Corned Beef and Cabbage

Ingredients:

1 3 lb. corned beef brisket with spice packet
1/2 small head cabbage, cut into 3 wedges
4 carrots, peeled, and cut into 2-inch pieces
1 onion, quartered
2 yellow potatoes, cut into 2-inch pieces
1/2 cup water

Directions:

1. Trim fat from brisket.
2. Cut brisket to fit into a 5- to 6-quart slow cooker.
3. Sprinkle spices from packet evenly over meat.
4. Rub the spices in with your fingers.
5. Place cabbage, carrots, onion, and potatoes in the slow cooker.
6. Pour water over vegetables.
7. Top with brisket.
8. Cover and cook on low-heat setting for 10 to 12 hours or on high-heat setting for 5 to 6 hours.
9. Transfer meat to a cutting board.
10. Thinly slice against the grain.
11. Serve vegetables with a slotted spoon.

Irish Soda Bread

Ingredients:

4 cups all-purpose flour
4 tbsps. white sugar
1 tsp. baking soda
1 tbsp. baking powder
1/2 tsp. salt
1/2 cup margarine, softened
1 cup buttermilk
1 egg
1/4 cup butter, melted
1/4 cup buttermilk

Directions:

1. Preheat oven to 375 degrees.
2. Lightly grease a large baking sheet.
3. In a large bowl, mix together flour, sugar, baking soda, baking powder, salt and margarine.
4. Stir in 1 cup of buttermilk and egg.
5. Turn dough out onto a lightly floured surface and knead slightly.
6. Form dough into a round and place on prepared baking sheet.
7. In a small bowl, combine melted butter with 1/4 cup buttermilk; brush loaf with this mixture. Use a sharp knife to cut an 'X' into the top of the loaf.
8. Bake in oven until a toothpick inserted into the center of the loaf comes out clean, 45 to 50 minutes.
9. Check for doneness after 30 minutes.
10. Brush the loaf with the butter mixture periodically while it bakes.

Irish Champ

Ingredients:

2 pounds potatoes, peeled and halved
1 cup milk
1 bunch green onions, thinly sliced
2 tsp. salt
1/4 cup butter
1 pinch freshly ground black pepper to taste

Directions:

1. Place potatoes into large pot, and fill with enough water to cover.
2. Bring to a boil.
3. Cook until tender (about 20 minutes).
4. Drain well.
5. Return to a low heat and let the potatoes sit while you do the next step.
6. Heat the milk and green onions gently in a saucepan, until warm.
7. Mash the potatoes, salt and butter together until smooth.
8. Stir in the milk and green onion until evenly mixed.
9. Season with freshly ground black pepper.
10. Serve with butter and enjoy!

Paddy's Colcannon

Ingredients:

4 peeled russet potatoes cut into large chunks
Salt
5-6 tbsps. unsalted butter
3 lightly packed cups of chopped kale, cabbage, chard, or other leafy greens
1/2 cup minced green onions minced (include the greens for color and flavor)
1 cup milk or cream

Directions:

1. Put the potatoes in a medium pot and cover with cold water by at least an inch.
2. Add 2 tbsps. of salt, and bring to a boil.
3. Boil until the potatoes are fork tender (15 to 20 minutes).
4. Drain in a colander.
5. Return the pot to the stove and set to medium-high heat.
6. Melt the butter.
7. Add the butter to the greens.
8. Cook the greens for 3-4 minutes, or until they are wilted.
9. Add the green onions and cook 1 minute more.
10. Pour in the milk or cream.
11. Mix well.
12. Add the potatoes.
13. Reduce the heat to medium.
14. Using a fork or potato masher, mash the potatoes, mixing them up with the greens.
15. Add salt to taste and serve hot.
16. Serve with a pat of butter in the center.

Emerald Isle Shepherd's Pie

Ingredients:

5 large potatoes - peeled and cubed
1/2 cup milk
1 tbsp. butter
1 lb. lean ground beef
1 onion, chopped
1 clove garlic, chopped
1 oz. margarine
1 oz. all-purpose flour
2 tbsps. ketchup
2 cups beef consommé
2 tbsps. browning and seasoning sauce
8 oz. shredded Cheddar cheese

Directions:

1. Place the potatoes in a pot with enough water to cover.
2. Bring to a boil and cook until tender. Drain and mash with desired amounts of milk and butter. Set aside.
3. While the potatoes are cooking, crumble the ground beef into a large skillet over medium heat.
4. Add onion and garlic; cook and stir until meat is no longer pink.
5. Preheat the oven to 400 degrees F (200 degrees C).
6. Melt the margarine in a small pan. Stir in the flour.
7. Cook and stir over medium heat until dark brown, about 10 minutes.
8. Let cool off the heat then gradually stir in the consommé, ketchup and browning sauce until smooth.
9. Set over medium heat and simmer until thick.
10. Stir the sauce into the ground beef and transfer to a casserole dish.
11. Top with mashed potato,.
12. Sprinkle the cheese over the potato.
13. Bake for 15 to 20 minutes in the preheated oven, until potatoes are toasted and cheese is melted.

Irish Lamb Stew

Ingredients:

1/3 cup plus 1 tbsp. all-purpose flour, divided
1-1/2 pounds lamb stew meat, cut into 1-inch cubes
3 tbsps. olive oil, divided
3 med. onions, chopped
3 garlic cloves, minced
4 cups reduced-sodium beef broth
2 med. potatoes, peeled and cubed
4 med. carrots, cut into 1-inch pieces
1 cup frozen peas
1 tsp. salt
1 tsp. dried thyme
1/2 tsp. pepper
1/2 tsp. Worcestershire sauce
2 tbsps. water

Directions:

1. Place 1/3 cup flour in a large re-sealable plastic bag.
2. Add lamb and shake to coat.
3. In a Dutch oven, brown lamb in batches in 2 tbsps. oil.
4. Remove and set aside.
5. In the same pan, sauté onions in remaining oil until tender.
6. Add garlic and cook 1 minute longer.
7. Add broth, stirring to loosen browned bits from pan.
8. Return lamb to the pan.
9. Bring to a boil.
10. Reduce heat; cover and simmer for 1 hour or until meat is tender.
11. Add potatoes and carrots; cover and cook for 20 minutes.
12. Stir in peas; cook 5-10 minutes longer or until vegetables are tender.
13. Add seasonings and Worcestershire sauce.
14. Combine remaining flour with water until smooth; stir into stew. Bring to a boil; cook and stir for 2 minutes or until thickened.
15. Serve and enjoy!

Potato Cakes

Ingredients:

1 lb. cooled mashed potatoes
1 egg, slightly beaten
Salt & freshly ground Black Pepper
1 cup all-purpose flour
2 scallions, finely chopped
1 tbsp. oil
Butter for serving

Directions:

1. Place the mashed potato in a large bowl.
2. Season with salt and pepper.
3. Add the egg.
4. Stir in the flour and combine well to form a dough.
5. Transfer the dough onto a floured work surface and lightly knead.
6. Roll out the dough to about 1 1/2 inch thick.
7. Cut into circles using a pastry cutter making approximately 8 potato cakes.
8. Place the oil into a pan and place over a medium heat.
9. Add the potato cakes and cook for about 3 minutes on each side or until golden brown.
10. Serve hot with a pat of butter on top.

Emerald Isle Beef in Guinness

Ingredients:

2 1/2 lb. shin of beef
2 large onions
6 medium carrots
2 tbsp. seasoned flour
a little fat or beef dripping
1/2 cup dry cider
1 cup Guinness with water (1/2 pint)
sprig of parsley

Directions:

1. Cut the beef into chunks and peel and slice the onions and carrots.
2. Toss the beef in the flour and brown quickly in hot fat.
3. Remove the beef and fry the onions gently until transparent.
4. Return the beef and add the carrots and the liquid.
5. Bring just to the boil, reduce the heat to a very gentle simmer, cover closely and cook for 1 1/2 - 2 hours.
6. Check that the dish does not dry out, adding more liquid if necessary.
7. Sprinkle with chopped parsley and serve with plainly boiled potatoes.

Gooseberry Crumble

Ingredients:

2 cups self-rising flour
1/2 cup brown sugar
1/2 cup butter
10 cups gooseberries
1 cup caster sugar

Directions:

1. Preheat oven to 350 degrees.
2. Using your fingertips, rub butter lightly into the flour in a large bowl.
3. When the texture resembles fine breadcrumbs, mix in the brown sugar.
4. Remove the stems and tops of the berries.
5. Cover with the crumble mixture in an oven-proof dish, pressing the surface down lightly.
6. Bake for 45 minutes in the center of oven.
7. Serve hot with cream.

Dublin Coddle

Ingredients:

1 lb. Irish sausages
1 lb. bacon
1 lb. potatoes, peeled and cut into large dice
2 large onions, roughly chopped
6 carrots, roughly chopped
1 quart chicken stock
1 quart whole milk
salt and pepper to taste

Directions:

1. Place a large Dutch oven over medium-high heat.
2. Cook the sausages and bacon in the bottom of the Dutch oven until the bacon is crisp.
3. Drain fat from the pan, reserving 1 tbsp. of drippings.
4. Crumble the bacon and halve the sausages.
5. Heat the reserved drippings to the Dutch oven over low heat along with the crumbled bacon and sausages.
6. Add the onions and carrots; cook and stir until the onions soften, 7 to 10 minutes.
7. Stir in the stock and milk; bring to a simmer until the potatoes are fork tender 30 to 45 minutes.
8. Season with salt and pepper to serve.

Potato Casserole

Ingredients:

8 to 10 medium potatoes
8 oz. cream cheese, softened
8 oz. sour cream
1/2 c melted butter
1/4 c chopped chives
1 clove garlic, minced
2 tsp salt
Dash paprika

Directions:

1. Cook, drain, and mash potatoes.
2. Beat cream cheese and sour cream together until smooth.
3. Add potatoes and all remaining ingredients, and then beat until combined.
4. Spoon into lightly buttered two-quart casserole, cover and refrigerate.
5. Remove from refrigerator 15 minutes before baking.
6. Uncover and sprinkle paprika on top (if desired).
7. Bake uncovered at 350 degrees about 40 minutes, or until thoroughly heated.

Fried Cabbage and Bacon

Ingredients:

1 (12 oz.) package bacon
1/4 cup bacon drippings
1 small head cabbage, cored and finely chopped
ground black pepper to taste

Directions:

1. Cook bacon in a deep skillet over medium heat until crisp, 5 to 7 minutes.
2. Remove bacon from skillet and drain on a paper towel-lined plate. Reserve 1/4 cup drippings in skillet.
3. Cook and stir cabbage in hot bacon drippings over medium heat until cabbage wilts, 5 to 7 minutes.
4. Crumble bacon over cabbage.
5. Stir and simmer until bacon is warmed, 2 to 3 minutes.
6. Season with black pepper.

Potato Soup

Ingredients:

6 medium potatoes
2 medium onions
6 cups stock or milk and water mixed
1 tbsps. butter
Parsley
Salt and pepper

Directions:

1. Peel and dice the potatoes.
2. Chop the onions.
3. Melt the butter and gently cook the onions and potatoes in a covered saucepan until soft but not colored.
4. Add the liquid.
5. Salt and pepper to taste.
6. Serve in bowls with a little chopped parsley sprinkled on top.

Irish Boxty

Ingredients:

1 cup raw potato
1 cup mashed potato
2 cups plain flour
1 tsp baking powder
1 tsp salt
large knob of butter, melted
1/2 cup milk

Directions:

1. Grate the raw potatoes into a bowl.
2. Turn out onto a cloth and wring, catching the liquid.
3. This will separate into a clear fluid with starch at the bottom.
4. Pour off the fluid and scrape out the starch and mix with the grated and mashed potatoes.
5. Sieve the dry ingredients and mix in along with the melted butter.
6. Add a little milk if necessary to make a pliable dough.
7. Knead lightly on a floured surface. Divide into four and form large, flat cakes.
8. Mark each into quarters but do not cut right through.
9. Bake on a griddle or in a heavy pan.

Guinness Mustard

Ingredients:

1/2 cup coarse-grained Dijon mustard
2 tbsps. regular Dijon mustard
2 tbsps. Guinness stout or other stout or porter
1 tbsp. minced shallot
1 tsp. golden brown sugar

Directions:

1. Whisk all ingredients in a small bowl to blend.
2. Cover and refrigerate at least 2 hours.

Dublin Iced Coffee

Ingredients:

2 oz. strong cold-brew coffee
2 oz. stout beer
1½ oz. Irish whiskey
¾ oz. simple syrup
1/2 oz. heavy cream
  Freshly grated cinnamon stick (for garnish)

Directions:

1. Mix coffee, stout, whiskey, and simple syrup in a highball glass.
2. Add ice to fill.
3. Gently pour in cream so it gradually sinks into coffee.
4. Sprinkle with cinnamon.

Dublin Lawyer

Ingredients:

1/2 cup (1 stick) unsalted butter, softened
1 tsp. cayenne
2 tsps. paprika
1 1/2 cups sliced button mushrooms
1/2 cup sliced scallions
1 lb. cooked lobster meat
Salt and freshly ground black pepper
1/4 cup Irish whiskey
4 cups heavy cream
2 cups hot cooked rice

Directions:

1. In a small mixing bowl thoroughly combine softened butter, cayenne pepper, and paprika.
2. In a large deep-sided skillet over medium-high heat, melt the cayenne butter and add the mushrooms, scallions and lobster meat.
3. Sauté until mushroom are golden, about 5 minutes, and season with salt and pepper, to taste.
4. Carefully add the whiskey off the heat and cook until almost completely evaporated.
5. Add the cream and reduce until thickened.
6. Serve in large bowls over hot rice.

Irish Cabbage Rolls

Ingredients:

10 cabbage leaves, blanched
1 lb. corned beef, roughly chopped
1 medium onion, quartered
1 stalk celery, cut into 1-inch pieces
1 egg, beaten slightly
1 cup cooked brown rice
2 tsps. spicy brown mustard
1 beef bouillon cube
¼ cup boiling water
1 (12 oz.) can beer
1 tbsp. butter
1 tbsp. flour

Directions:

1. Preheat oven to 350 degrees.
2. Place corned beef in a food processor and chop finely.
3. Set aside.
4. Add onion and celery and finely chop.
5. In a bowl, combine egg, rice and mustard.
6. Mix in corned beef, onion, and celery.
7. Place 1/2 cup on each cabbage leaf and roll up tucking in ends.
8. Place seam side down in a 13x9 inch baking pan.
9. Dissolve bouillon in boiling water.
10. Add beer and pour over cabbage rolls.
11. Cover tightly and bake 1 1/2 hours.
12. Remove from oven and pour out 1 cup of liquid.
13. Melt butter in a saucepan, add flour, stir and cook over low heat 1 minute.
14. Add liquid, increase heat to medium high, bring to a boil, reduce heat and simmer until thickened.
15. Pour over cabbage rolls and serve with additional mustard.

Colcannon Bake

Ingredients:

3 potatoes, peeled and quartered
1 pinch salt
6 tbsps. butter, cut into small chunks
1/2 cup sour cream 1 egg
1 tbsp. milk, or as needed
1 tsp. butter, or as needed
3 cups shredded cabbage
2 leeks, chopped
1 small onion, chopped
2 cubes chicken bouillon
1/2 cup shredded Cheddar cheese

Directions:

1. Place the potatoes into a large pot and cover with salted water.
2. Bring to a boil, then reduce heat to medium-low, cover, and simmer until tender, about 20 minutes.
3. Drain and allow to steam dry for a minute or two. Season the potatoes with salt, and mash with 6 tbsps. of butter, sour cream, egg, and milk.
4. Preheat oven to 350 degrees F (175 degrees C).
5. Grease a 2-quart casserole.
6. Heat 1 tsp. butter in a skillet over medium heat, and cook and stir the cabbage, leeks, and onion until the cabbage is tender and the onion is translucent, about 10 minutes.
7. Crush 2 bouillon cubes into the cabbage mixture, and stir to blend and dissolve the cubes.
8. Stir the cabbage mixture into the potato mixture until thoroughly mixed, and spoon into the prepared casserole.
9. Bake in the preheated oven for 40 minutes.
10. Top with Cheddar cheese, and return to oven until the cheese melts, about 10 minutes.

Irish Liver and Onions

Ingredients:

1 tsp. olive oil, or more if needed
1 clove garlic, minced
4 large sweet onions, thinly sliced
1 1/2 tbsps. finely chopped green bell pepper
1 1/2 tbsps. finely chopped red bell pepper
1/2 cup sliced fresh mushrooms
Salt and black pepper to taste
1/4 cup butter
1 lb. calf's liver, skinned, deveined, and sliced
1/4 cup all-purpose flour
2 cups cold water
2 tsps. beef bouillon granules
1 tbsp. red wine

Directions:

1. Heat the olive oil in a large skillet over medium heat. Stir in the garlic, onion, green bell pepper, red bell pepper, and mushrooms.
2. Cook and stir until the onion has softened and turned translucent, about 5 minutes.
3. Season with salt and pepper.
4. Push onion mixture to the side of the skillet, and place the butter in the center of the skillet. Add calf's liver, one slice at a time.
5. Cover and cook until lightly browned, flipping liver slices once, 5 to 6 minutes.
6. Cut liver slices in half.
7. Whisk together flour, water, and beef bouillon in a bowl until combined.
8. Pour mixture into the skillet; cook and stir until gravy thickens, then add red wine.
9. Cook for 2 more minutes. Remove from heat and serve.

Irish Heritage Cabbage

Ingredients:

2 slices Irish bacon, diced
1 medium head cabbage, cored and cut into wedges
2 tbsps. melted butter
2 tsps. ground nutmeg
2 cups water
salt and pepper to taste
1/2 cup red wine vinega

Directions:

1. Preheat your oven's broiler.
2. Place cabbage into a large pot.
3. Add water and bring to a boil.
4. Simmer over low heat until tender, about 15 minutes.
5. Meanwhile, cook bacon in a skillet over medium-high heat until crisp.
6. Drain and set aside.
7. Drain cabbage, and drizzle with melted butter. Sprinkle with bacon and nutmeg.
8. Transfer to a baking dish.
9. Place under your oven's broiler until the top layer is lightly browned, about 5 minutes.
10. Serve with salt, pepper and vinegar as desired.

Irish Corn O'Brien

Ingredients:

2 slices bacon, cut into
1/2 inch pieces
1/4 cup minced white onion
2 tbsps. green bell pepper, chopped
2 cups whole kernel corn, drained
1 tbsp. chopped pimento peppers
Salt and pepper to taste

Directions:

1. Place the bacon in a large, deep skillet, and cook over medium heat, stirring until evenly browned, about 10 minutes.
2. Drain the bacon on a paper towel-lined plate, leaving the grease in the skillet.
3. Stir the onion and bell pepper into the skillet, and cook until the onion has softened and turned translucent, about 5 minutes.
4. Add the corn, pimentos, and reserved bacon.
5. Cook and stir until heated through, 3 to 5 minutes.
6. Season with salt and pepper before serving.

Irish Scalloped Potatoes

Ingredients:

6 potatoes, peeled and thinly sliced
1/2 cup butter, cut into thin slices
salt and ground black pepper to taste
1 pint half-and-half

Directions:

1. Preheat oven to 325 degrees F (165 degrees C).
2. Arrange thinly sliced potatoes in a 9x13-inch baking dish.
3. Layer butter slices on top of potatoes.
4. Season with salt and black pepper.
5. Pour half-and-half evenly over potato mixture.
6. Bake in preheated oven until sauce has thickened and potatoes are tender, 45 to 60 minutes.

Irish Quick Hoppin' John

Ingredients:

1 c. long-grain white rice
2 tbsp. olive oil
6 oz. andouille sausage, sliced into half-moons
1 medium onion, chopped
1 medium green pepper, cut into 1/4-in. pieces
1 large clove garlic, finely chopped
1 jalapeno, thinly sliced
2 15-oz. cans black-eyed peas
3 c. baby spinach

Directions:

1. Cook the rice according to package directions.
2. Meanwhile, heat 1 tbsp. oil in a large skillet over medium-high heat.
3. Add the sausage and cook, tossing once, until browned, 2 to 3 minutes.
4. Transfer to a bowl.
5. Return the pan to medium heat and heat the remaining tbsp. oil.
6. Add the onion and cook, covered, for 4 minutes.
7. Add the pepper and cook, stirring occasionally, until the vegetables are tender, 5 to 6 minutes.
8. Stir in the garlic and jalapeno and cook for 1 minute.
9. Add the beans and 1/2 cup water and cook until heated through.
10. Return the sausage to the skillet along with the spinach and cook until beginning to wilt, about 2 minutes.
11. Serve over the rice.

Irish Soda Farls

Ingredients:

2 cups all-purpose flour
1/2 tsp. salt
1 tsp. baking soda
1 cup buttermilk

Directions:

1. Preheat heavy based flat griddle or skillet on medium to low heat.
2. Placc flour and salt in a bowl and sift in baking soda.
3. Make a well in the center, and pour in the buttermilk.
4. Work quickly to mix into dough and knead very lightly on a well floured surface.
5. Form into a flattened circle, about 1/2 inch thick and cut into quarters with a floured knife.
6. Sprinkle a little flour over the base of the hot pan and cook the farls for 6 to 8 minutes on each side or until golden brown.

Cornbread and Beef Skillet Pie

Ingredients:

1 lb. Lean Ground Beef
1 can Ranchero Beans
1 can corn kernels
1 package cornbread mix (plus the required ingredients to make it)
2 oz. pepperjack cheese

Directions:

1. Heat oven to 400 degrees F.
2. In a large oven-safe skillet, cook beef over medium-high heat, breaking it up with the back of a spoon until browned, 5 to 7 minutes.
3. Stir in the beans and corn and cook simmer for 2 minutes.
4. Meanwhile, prepare the cornbread according to package directions.
5. Spread the cornbread batter over the beef mixture, leaving a 1/2-inch border all the way around. Sprinkle with cheese.
6. Bake until golden brown and a toothpick inserted into the cornbread comes out clean, 15 to 20 minutes. Let cool for 5 minutes before serving.

Sweet Potato Corned Beef Hash

Ingredients:

2 medium white potatoes, diced
1/2 large sweet potato, diced
1 tsp salt
1 tbsp butter
1/2 onion, diced
1/4 cup corned beef juice, or more if needed
1-1/2 cups of diced corned beef
1/4 tsp paprika
Eggs if desired

Directions:

1. Cut and peel 2 cups of white diced potatoes and 2 cups of sweet potatoes (this will equal to about 2 medium white potatoes and a half of one large sweet potato).
2. Rinse the potatoes well then add to a large pot of water.
3. Add 1 tsp of salt to the water and boil on high for 15 minutes until potatoes are just cooked.
4. Drain and set aside.
5. In a large frying pan add butter and melt on medium heat then add 3 tbsps. of corned beef juice.
6. Add 1/2 onion diced and diced corned beef.
7. Simmer on low for 5 minutes.
8. Add potato mixture and paprika to the pan.
9. Bump the heat up to high and cook for 5 minutes (keeping the potato mixture on top).
10. Mix the potatoes with the meat and flip over.
11. Smash down with a spatula and cook for an additional 5 minutes.
12. Add the remaining one tbsp. of corned beef juice and more butter if needed.
13. Cook for 5 minutes more (the hash should be crispy but not burnt).
14. Serve with or without a fried egg on top.

Irish Nachos

Ingredients:

4 large Red Skinned Potatoes
3 tbsps. Extra Virgin Olive Oil
2 tsps. Garlic Powder
2 tsps. Sweet Paprika
1/2 Red Bell Pepper
1/2 Yellow Bell Pepper
1 medium Yellow Onion
Coarse Salt to taste
Freshly ground Black Pepper to taste
5 strips Bacon
1 cup shredded Cheddar Cheese
2 Hass Avocados
1 tbsp. Lemon Juice
1/2 cup thinly sliced Scallions
Sour Cream, for serving
Salsa, for serving

Directions:

1. Preheat the oven to 400 degrees F with the rack in the middle.
2. Carefully cut the potatoes into 1/4 inch slices.
3. Rinse them in cold water and dry both sides with a clean dish towel.
4. Add the potatoes to a large bowl, drizzle with 2 tbsps. of the olive oil, garlic powder and paprika. Toss to combine. Arrange the slices partly overlapping one another in a 12 inch cast iron skillet.
5. Transfer the skillet to the oven and bake potatoes for 40 minutes, until golden brown and cooked through.
6. While the potatoes are baking, thinly slice the red pepper, yellow pepper and onion into 1/4 inch pieces. Add the remaining 1 tbsp. of olive oil to a large skillet over medium high heat. Add the peppers and onions. Cook stirring occasionally, until the onions are translucent ~ about 5 minutes. Remove the mixture from the skillet & set aside.
7. Add the bacon to the skillet and reduce the heat to medium. Cook the bacon until golden brown and slightly crisp, turning half way through. Transfer the bacon to a paper towel-lined plate and let cool. Break the bacon into 1 inch pieces and set aside.
8. Once the potatoes are cooked, remove the skillet from the oven and add the pepper & onion mixture on top of the potatoes, followed by the cheese.

9. Transfer the skillet back to the oven for 5 minutes to melt the cheese.
10. Once the cheese has melted, remove the skillet from the oven and sprinkle the bacon on top.
1. Cut each avocado in 1/2 lengthwise.
2. Remove the pit from the avocado and discard.
3. Scoop the avocado flesh from the skin, and place the avocado flesh in a medium bowl.
4. Mash the avocado together with the scallions and lemon juice, season with salt and pepper.
5. Add the mashed avocado on top of the nachos and serve immediately with sour cream & salsa.

Green Silver Dollar Pancakes

Ingredients:

Pancakes
1 cup plain or buttermilk pancake mix
1 large egg
3/4 cup milk
3 tbsp. butter
1 tbsp. granulated sugar
green food coloring
Topping
4 tbsp. cream cheese
3 tbsp. confectioners' sugar
2 tbsp. milk
1 c. Lucky Charms (cereal and marshmallow pieces)

Directions:

1. Preheat oven to 250 degrees F.
2. Place cookie sheet in oven.
3. In large bowl, whisk pancake milk, egg, milk, butter, granulated sugar, and green food coloring until combined with a few lumps.
4. Lightly grease a griddle or 12-inch, nonstick skillet.
5. Heat on medium heat until very hot.
6. Drop rounded teaspoonfuls of batter onto hot griddle.
7. Cook for 2 to 3 minutes, or until cooked through, flipping once.
8. Transfer to cookie sheet in the oven to keep warm.
9. In medium bowl, with hand-mixer on medium, beat cream cheese, confectioners' sugar, and milk until smooth.
10. Serve silver dollar pancakes topped with cream cheese glaze and Lucky Charms.

Chocolate Stout Crepes with Irish Cream Whip

Ingredients:

For Crepes:
1/2 cup Whole Wheat Flour
1/2 cup All Purpose Flour
1 Tbsp Sugar
1/4 tsp Salt
3 whole Eggs
1/2 cup Milk
2 tsp Cocoa Powder
1/2 tsp Vanilla Extract
2 tsp Canola or Vegetable Oil
1/2 cup Stout Beer
For Cream Filling:
1 cup Heavy Whipping Cream
2 Tbsp Fine Grain Sugar
2 Tbsp Irish Cream

Directions:

1. In stand mixer with whisk attachment, beat together flours, sugar, salt, milk, eggs, vanilla, cocoa powder, and oil. Whisk on medium-high until nearly all clumps are gone and mixture is smooth. Place in bowl and refrigerate for at least 30 minutes, or up to overnight if you wish.
2. When ready to make, pour in 1/2 cup of Stout Beer and whisk until just incorporated.
3. Coat a 10" non-stick skillet with non-stick spray and heat over medium-high heat.
4. Pour in 1/3 cup of batter.
5. Immediately tilt and rotate pan evenly distributing batter along the entire bottom of the pan.
6. Cook until under side is lightly browned, or about 1-1 1/2 minutes. Gently flip crepe with spatula and continue to cook an additional 45 seconds. Slide onto a plate and allow to cool.
7. Repeat the process with the remaining batter.
8. Using a cleaned stand mixer bowl and whisk attachment, beat together heavy whipping cream, fine grain sugar and Irish Cream until stiff peaks form in the whipped cream.

9. When crepes have cooled, dollop whipped cream into middle of each crepe and roll the crepes to close them. They can also be folded into quarters. Serve immediately with a dash of powdered sugar on top.

Irish Wheaten Bread

Ingredients:

1 cup bread flour
2 3/4 cups whole wheat flour
1 1/4 tsps. salt
1 1/4 tsps. baking soda
2 tsps. white sugar
1/4 cup margarine
2 cups buttermilk
1/4 cup vegetable oil
1 tbsp. buttermilk
1 tsp. white sugar

Directions:

1. Preheat oven to 400 degrees F (200 degrees C).
2. Prepare a shallow baking pan with cooking spray.
3. Sift together the bread flour, whole wheat flour, salt, baking soda, and 2 tsps. sugar in a bowl.
4. Cut the margarine into the flour mixture until pieces are nearly indistinguishable.
5. Make a well in the center of the mixture and pour in the oil and buttermilk.
6. Stir with a spatula until dry mixture is completely moistened.
7. Move the dough to a lightly-floured surface.
8. Lightly knead the dough for no more than 1 minute.
9. Place the dough into the prepared pan; pat down and around to form a round loaf.
10. Cut a cross into the top of the loaf with your finger.
11. Brush the top with 1 tbsp. buttermilk; sprinkle 1 tsp. sugar over the top of the loaf.
12. Bake in the preheated oven for 30 minutes.
13. Reduce heat to 375 degrees F (190 degrees C); rotate pan and bake another 30 minutes.
14. Allow loaf to cool on a wire rack before slicing.

Guinness Beef Stew

Ingredients:

2 tbsp. olive oil
2½ lb. lean beef stew meat
kosher salt
Pepper
2 tbsp. all-purpose flour
2 c. stout beer
1 can tomato paste
3 medium onions
4 clove garlic
8 sprig fresh thyme
1 small rutabaga
4 medium carrots
2 medium parsnips
½ c. chopped fresh flat-leaf parsley
mashed potatoes

Directions:

1. Heat oil in a large skillet over medium-high heat.
2. Season the beef with 1/2 tsp. each salt and pepper.
3. Working in batches, cook beef, turning occasionally, until browned, 4 to 5 minutes; transfer to a plate and sprinkle with flour.
4. In a 5- to 6-quart slow cooker, whisk together beer, tomato paste, and 1/4 tsp. each salt and pepper.
5. Add onions, garlic, thyme, and beef and any juices, and toss to combine. Scatter rutabaga, carrots and parsnips on top.
6. Cook, covered, until beef and vegetables are tender and sauce has slightly thickened, 7 to 8 hours on low or 5 to 6 hours on high.
7. Gently fold in parsley and serve with mashed potatoes, if desired.

Irish Potato Bread

Ingredients
½ lb. of cooked potatoes
1 oz. butter
½ tea spoon of salt
Around 2 oz. of flour (until pliable dough)

Directions:

1. Peel and cut the potatoes small then boil the until soft
2. Drain the water
3. Add the butter (while still warm)
4. Add the salt (while still warm)
5. Mash or put through a ricer until no lumps
6. Work in the flour until you have a pliable and then stiff enough dough. you my noy use it all
7. Place some flour on a flat surface and flour your hands or it will get sticky
8. Roll the dough into a circle 1 cm or 1/3 of an inch thick
9. Cut into traditional squares, rectangles or triangles.
10. Cook in a pre-heated frying pan.
11. Cook until golden brown on both sides.
12. They should be like a patchy effect when nearly done.

Irish Veda Bread

Ingredients:

1 tbsp. brown sugar
3 tbsp. malt extract
2 tbsp. black treacle
1oz butter, plus extra for greasing
12oz strong white bread flour, plus extra for flouring
3½oz strong wholemeal flour
1 pinch salt
½oz fast action yeast
8oz sultanas
9 fl. oz. warm water
1 tbsp. warm honey, to glaze

Directions:

1. Place the sugar, malt extract, treacle and butter in a pan and heat gently until the butter has melted and the sugar has dissolved.
2. Leave to cool.
3. Mix the flours, salt, yeast and sultanas in a mixing bowl.
4. Pour in the cooled malt syrup mixture and the warm water.
5. Mix thoroughly; the mixture will be soft and sticky.
6. Turn the mixture onto a floured surface and knead gently for a few minutes to bring the mixture together.
7. Grease two 450g/1lb loaf tins and divide the mixture among them. Smooth the mixture with the back of a spoon so that the top is smooth and level. Cover each tin with a plastic bag so that it is loose and not touching the top of the tin.
8. Leave for a couple of hours, or until the dough has risen to the top of the tins.
9. Preheat the oven to 375 degrees F (190 degrees C.).
10. Remove the plastic bags and bake for 30-40 minutes.
11. If the top of the loaf starts to brown too quickly, cover with a sheet of foil and continue baking.
12. Remove from the oven and brush the top with warm honey to glaze.
13. Cool on a wire rack.
14. Slice and eat with butter.

Irish Beer Bread

Ingredients:

2.67 c. self-rising flour (not cake flour)
12 oz. beer, freshly opened

Directions:

1. Heat oven to 375°F. You'll need a 9 x 5 x 3-in. loaf pan, lightly greased.
2. Put flour in a medium bowl. Add beer and stir with a rubber spatula just until flour is moistened completely. Scrape into prepared pan.
3. Bake 50 to 55 minutes until top is lightly browned, the sides pull away from the pan and pick inserted near center comes out clean.
4. Cool in pan on a wire rack 5 minutes, then turn out on rack to cool.
5. Cut in 1/2-in. slices to serve. Makes great toast.

Irish Pork Chops with Cabbage and Apples

Ingredients:

1 tsp. oil
4 well-trimmed, 1-in.-thick
1 large Red Onion
4 c. Shredded green cabbage
½ c. each apple cider or juice
¼ tsp. each salt and pepper
¼ tsp. caraway seeds (optional)
1 Gala apple, quartered, cored, cut in ½-in.-thick wedges
2 tbsp. snipped fresh dill
2 tsp. cider vinegar

Directions:

1. Heat oil in a large nonstick skillet.
2. Add chops and cook, turning once, 5 minutes until browned.
3. Remove.
4. Add onion to skillet; sauté 3 minutes until golden.
5. Add cabbage, cider, broth, salt, pepper and caraway seeds; cook, stirring often, 5 minutes or until cabbage is almost tender.
6. Stir in apple; cook 3 minutes, stirring often, until apple is almost tender.
7. Place chops on top.
8. Cover and cook over low heat 2 minutes or until cabbage and apple are tender and chops are heated through. Remove chops to plates or platter.
9. Stir dill and vinegar into cabbage mixture. Serve with the chops.

Irish Breakfast Fry Up

Ingredients:

6 thick slices bacon
2 tbsps. butter or margarine
4 eggs
2 small tomatoes, sliced
1 1/2 cups whole mushrooms
4 slices prepared soda bread

Directions:

1. Lay the bacon slices in a single layer in a large skillet.
2. Fry over medium heat until it begins to get tinged with brown.
3. Fry on both sides. Remove from pan, but save grease.
4. Melt butter in skillet.
5. Crack eggs into pan, being careful not to break yolks.
6. Place tomato slices, mushrooms, and bread in pan.
7. Fry gently, stirring mushrooms and tomatoes occasionally.
8. Keep everything separate.
9. Turn bread over to brown on both sides.
10. When egg whites are set, but yolks are still runny, dish half of everything onto each of 2 warmed plates, and serve immediately.

Irish Fish and Chips

Ingredients:

4 large potatoes, peeled and cut into strips
1 cup all-purpose flour
1 tsp. baking powder
1 tsp. salt
1 tsp. ground black pepper
1 cup milk
1 egg
1 quart vegetable oil for frying
1 1/2 pounds cod fillets

Directions:

1. Place potatoes in a medium-size bowl of cold water. In a separate medium-size mixing bowl, mix together flour, baking powder, salt, and pepper. Stir in the milk and egg; stir until the mixture is smooth.
2. Let mixture stand for 20 minutes.
3. Preheat the oil in a large pot or electric skillet to 350 degrees F (175 degrees C).
4. Fry the potatoes in the hot oil until they are tender. Drain them on paper towels.
5. Dredge the fish in the batter, one piece at a time, and place them in the hot oil. Fry until the fish is golden brown.
6. If necessary, increase the heat to maintain the 350 degrees F (175 degrees C) temperature.
7. Drain well on paper towels.
8. Fry the potatoes again for 1 to 2 minutes for added crispness.

Irish Cheese and Bacon Potatoes

Ingredients:

1/2 lb. bacon
3 extra large russet potatoes, peeled and chopped into 1/2"-3/4" pieces
1 tsp. kosher salt
3/4 tsp. freshly ground black pepper
1 1/2 cups shredded cheddar or Mexican blend shredded cheeses
3 green onions, sliced thin

Directions:

1. Spread the bacon strips out across a large rimmed baking sheet pan and place on the middle rack of a COLD oven.
2. Set the temperature to 400 degrees. Set a timer for 16 minutes and check the bacon. Remove it from the oven when it is as crisp or crunchy as you like. I remove ours at 18 minutes and it's a great balance of chewy crunch. If you like your bacon crispy enough to crumble, you will probably want to cook it another minute past that.
3. While the bacon is cooking, peel and chop the potatoes.
4. Transfer the bacon to a paper towel lined plate to drain.
5. There should be 2-3 tbsps. of bacon grease left on the tray.
6. Put the potatoes on the tray and toss with tongs to thoroughly coat them in the bacon grease.
7. Sprinkle with salt and pepper.
8. Spread the potatoes out in a single layer and bake for 20 minutes, stir well and bake an additional 20 minutes.
9. Stir again, making sure that none of the potatoes are sticking to the tray. Bake another 15 minutes.
10. Chop the bacon into small pieces.
11. Remove the potatoes from the oven, stir again and sprinkle generously with shredded cheese and chopped bacon.
12. Return the tray to the oven and bake an additional 2-3 minutes, until the cheese has melted. Top with sliced green onions just before serving.

Irish Leprechaun Chow Snack Mix

Ingredients:

4 cups Lucky Charms (cereal and marshmallow bits)
4 cup Chex cereal
2 bar white chocolate
⅓ cup green sprinkles or sanding sugar

Directions:

1. Line a large jelly-roll pan with foil. Toss the Lucky Charms and Chex together on the pan until combined.
2. In a medium microwave-safe bowl, microwave the white chocolate in 30-second intervals, stirring, 1 minute or until melted.
3. Pour white chocolate over cereal, top with sprinkles, and toss to coat. Refrigerate for 15 minutes or until the chocolate sets. Break into pieces.

Irish Cornish Pastie

Ingredients:

2 unbaked pie crusts
1 medium potato (peeled and cubed into small cubes)
1 medium onion (chopped)
1 small rutabaga (uncooked, peeled and chopped)
½ lb of lean roast (cut into small cubes) or ½ lb steak (cut into small cubes)
1 tsp. salt
1 tsp. black pepper
1 small amount cold water

Directions:

1. Add the potato, onion, rutabega, meat and spices together and mix well.
2. Lay out one of the pie crusts and put half the ingredients on half of the pie crust leaving about 1 inch along the edge for sealing.
3. Lightly dampen along the edges of the pie crust with your fingertips.
4. Lay the other half of the pie crust over the top of the filling and press the top and bottom edges together well.
5. Fold the sealed edge toward the center and either crimp with your fingers or press along the entire folded edge with the tines of a fork.
6. Bake 425 degrees F. for 15 minutes then lower temperature to 350 degrees F for an additional 30 minutes.
7. Serve hot with brown or white gravy or serve cold without.

Irish Purple Cabbage & Pecan Salad

Ingredients:

1 head cabbage, shredded or
1 bag coleslaw mix, if you are in a hurry
1 cup Chinese pecans (sweetened pecans)
3 scallions, chopped including the green part

Directions:

1. Mix the dressing separately.
2. You can make the dressing in advance.
3. Just shake well and pour over the cabbage, pecans, and scallions.
4. Mix well to coat and serve immediately or else the pecans will start to soften.

Irish Black Pudding

Part of a traditional Irish breakfast.

Ingredients:

1 lb. cooked barley
1 lb. fresh beef suet
1 quarter pint fresh pig's blood (seriously)
8 oz. bread crumbs
8 oz. fine oatmeal
1/4 pint skimmed milk - warmed to room temperature
1 small onion - chopped
2 tsps. pepper
2 tsps. dried mint
1 and 1/2 tsp. salt
1/2 tsp. allspice

Directions:

1. Preheat oven to 350 degrees.
2. In a very large bowl, soak bread crumbs in the milk.
3. Add the blood and stir. Add cooked barely and stir.
4. Grate the beef suet into the bowl. Add the oatmeal and stir. Finally add onion and seasonings and stir once more.
5. Dived the mixture among two large roasting pans - filling them about 2/3 full.
6. Bake for one hour until the pudding is completely cooked.
7. Allow pudding to cool completely.
8. Cut into squares and fry in butter until the edges of both sides are crisp.
9. Serve as part of a traditional Irish breakfast.

Irish Crisp Sandwich

What Americans call "Potato Chips" the Irish call "Crisps."

Ingredients:

1 bag of crisps (potato chips)
Butter
2 Slices thick crusty bread.

Directions:

1. Cut the bread as thick as you like.
2. Slather one side of each slice with lots and lots of butter.
3. Pour the crisps on the buttered bread.
4. Smoosh it all together and enjoy!

Irish Soda Bread Pudding

Ingredients:

2 tbsps. unsalted butter, softened
8 eggs, beaten
1 cup heavy cream
1 orange, zested and juiced
1/2 cup light brown sugar
1 tsp. ground cinnamon
1 tsp. ground cardamom
1/2 tsp. vanilla extract
1/2 tsp. salt
1/2 recipe, Irish Soda Bread with Dried Blueberries, cubed and toasted
1/2 recipe cajeta or dulce de leche (about 1 cup)

Directions:

1. Preheat oven to 375°F.
2. Lightly grease a 9"x13" baking dish and set aside.
3. Place eggs, cream, orange zest, juice, sugar, cinnamon, cardamom, and salt in a mixing bowl and whisk together until fully combined.
4. Place cubes of bread into another mixing bowl and pour egg mixture over. Fold together until well combined.
5. Pour mixture into the prepared baking dish and allow mixture to sit for 30 minutes.
6. Place dish in the oven and bake for 30 to 40 minutes or until mixture has cooked through and is toasted on top, but soft and slightly custard-like in the center.
7. Top with 2/3 of the cajeta, allow the pudding to cool for 10-15 minutes and serve with extra sauce.

Irish Chicken and Dumplings

Ingredients:

2 (10.75 oz.) cans condensed cream of chicken soup
3 cups water
1 cup chopped celery
2 onions, quartered
1 tsp. salt
1/2 tsp. poultry seasoning
1/2 tsp. ground black pepper
4 skinless, boneless chicken breast halves
5 carrots, sliced
1 (10 oz.) package frozen green peas
4 potatoes, quartered
3 cups baking mix
1 1/3 cups milk

Directions:

1. In large, heavy pot, combine soup, water, chicken, celery, onion, salt, poultry seasoning, and pepper.
2. Cover and cook over low heat about 1 1/2 hours.
3. Add potatoes and carrots; cover and cook another 30 minutes.
4. Remove chicken from pot, shred it, and return to pot.
5. Add peas and cook only 5 minutes longer.
6. Add dumplings.

Dumplings Irections:

1. Mix baking mix and milk until a soft dough forms.
2. Drop by tablespoonfuls onto boiling stew.
3. Simmer covered for 10 minutes, then uncover and simmer an additional 10 minutes.

Irish Chicken and Leek Pie

Ingredients:

1 pastry for a 9 inch single crust pie
1 (4 lb.) whole chicken, deboned and cut into bite size pieces
4 slices cooked ham
4 leeks, chopped
1 onion, chopped salt and pepper to taste
1 pinch ground mace
1 1/4 cups chicken stock
1 tbsp. milk
1/2 cup heavy cream

Directions:

1. Preheat the oven to 350 degrees F (175 degrees C).
2. In a 1 1/2 quart casserole dish, layer the chicken, ham, leeks and onion a couple of times each until the dish is full. Season each layer with a little salt, pepper and mace. Pour the chicken stock over the layers, and dampen the edges of the dish.
3. Roll the pie pastry out large enough to cover the top of the dish, and place over the top. Crimp the sides down with a fork, and trim the excess from the edges. Cut a round hole in the center of the pastry. Roll dough scraps out and cut into strips. Use the strips to form a design, and place lightly over the hole. Brush the entire top with milk.
4. Bake for 35 to 45 minutes in the preheated oven, until chicken is cooked through.
5. If the top crust is getting too brown, cover it with parchment or aluminum foil.
6. While the pie is baking, heat the cream over low heat.
7. When the pie is cooked, remove from the oven, and carefully remove the design from the hole.
8. Pour the cream into the hole, and replace the design. Let stand for a few minutes before serving.

Irish Root Soup

Ingredients:

1/4 cup butter
1 large yellow onion, chopped
2 leeks, white and pale-green parts only, coarsely chopped
4 cloves garlic, smashed
1 stalk celery, cut into chunks
4 cups vegetable stock
5 potatoes, peeled and cubed
1 cup vegetable stock
1 1/4 cups sliced baby carrots
3 tbsps. chopped green onion
3/4 cup heavy cream salt and ground black pepper to taste
6 tbsps. shredded Cheddar cheese

Directions:

1. Melt the butter in a large stockpot over medium heat; cook and stir the onion, leeks, garlic, and celery in the melted butter until tender, about 10 minutes.
2. Pour 4 cups vegetable stock into the stockpot; add the potatoes.
3. Bring the mixture to a boil, reduce heat to medium-low, and cook the mixture at a simmer 20 minutes.
4. Divide the stock mixture into 3 batches with equal amounts of liquid and vegetables; set aside to cool for 30 minutes.
5. Pour 1 batch of the stock mixture into a blender, filling the pitcher no more than halfway. Hold the blender lid firmly in place and carefully start the blender.
6. Use a few quick pulses to get the mixture moving before leaving it on to puree.
7. Repeat process with second batch.
8. Return the pureed batches to the stockpot.
9. Divide third batch into two equal batches. Puree only one of the two batches before returning both to the stockpot.
10. Bring 1 cup vegetable stock to a simmer in a small pot over medium-low heat.
11. Cook the carrots in the simmering stock until soft, 5 to 7 minutes; add to the puree in the stockpot.
12. Stir the green onion and heavy cream through the puree; continue cooking another 5 minutes.
13. Season with salt and pepper; top with Cheddar cheese to serve.

Irish Soda Bread Cookies

Ingredients:

2 cups all-purpose flour
3/4 cup white sugar
1/2 tsp. baking soda
1/2 cup butter
1/2 cup dried currants
1/4 cup buttermilk 1 egg
1/4 tsp. salt
1 tsp. caraway seed

Directions:

1. Preheat oven to 350 degrees F (175 degrees C).
2. Combine dry ingredients in a mixing bowl.
3. With a pastry blender, cut in butter until mixture resembles coarse meal. Stir in currants.
4. Mix in beaten egg.
5. Pour in milk and mix with a fork to make a soft dough (may need a little more milk).
6. On a floured surface, shape dough into a ball and knead lightly 5 or 6 times.
7. Roll out dough to 1/4 inch thick and cut into squares and triangles with a knife (approximately 2 inches in diameter).
8. Bake for 12 to 14 minutes or until slightly browned.

Irish Cream Sugar Cookies

Ingredients:

1 cup butter, softened
1 1/2 cups white sugar
1 tsp. vanilla extract
1 egg yolk
1 egg
1/2 cup Irish cream liqueur
4 cups all-purpose flour
1/2 tsp. salt
1 tbsp. baking powder

Directions:

1. Cream together butter and sugar until fluffy.
2. Beat in vanilla and egg yolk until combined, then beat in egg.
3. Beat until smooth. Pour in Irish cream, and beat until incorporated.
4. Sift together flour, salt, and baking powder.
5. Stir into butter mixture until evenly mixed.
6. Form into a flattened ball, wrap well with plastic wrap, and refrigerate 2 hours to overnight.
7. Preheat oven to 350 degrees F (175 degrees C).
8. Line two baking sheets with parchment paper.
9. Roll dough out to 1/4 inch thickness on a floured work surface.
10. Cut into shapes using cookie cutters and place onto prepared baking sheets.
11. Bake in preheated oven until golden brown around the edges, 6 to 8 minutes. Cool on a wire rack until they reach room temperature.

Irish Shamrock Cookies

Ingredients:

1/2 cup butter, softened
1 (3 oz.) package instant pistachio pudding mix
1 1/3 cups baking mix
1 egg
1 tbsp. white sugar

Directions:

1. Preheat oven to 350 degrees F (175 degrees C).
2. Lightly grease baking sheet.
3. Cream together the butter or margarine and the pudding mix.
4. Blend in the baking mix, egg and sugar and mix well.
5. On a lightly floured surface roll out the dough to 3/8 inch thickness and cut into cookies with a shamrock cookie cutter.
6. Place cookies on the prepared baking sheet and bake at 350 degrees F (175 degrees C) for 9 to 10 minutes or until lightly browned on the edges. Let cookies cool on rack.
7. Frost with green colored icing if desired.

Irish Flag Cookies

Ingredients:

1 cup butter
1 1/2 cups confectioners' sugar
1 egg
1 tsp. vanilla extract
2 1/2 cups all-purpose flour
1 tsp. baking soda
1 tsp. cream of tartar

Directions:

1. In a large bowl, cream together butter and confectioners' sugar.
2. Beat in egg and vanilla extract. Mix well.
3. In a medium sized bowl, stir together the flour, baking soda and cream of tartar.
4. Blend into the butter mixture. Divide dough into thirds and shape into balls.
5. Working with 1/3 of the dough at a time, roll out dough to 1/4 inch thick on a floured surface.
6. With a knife, cut dough into rectangles about 2 inches high by 3 inches long. (6 x 8 cm).
7. Place rectangles on an ungreased cookie sheet, 2 inches apart. Bake in a preheated 350 degree F (175 degrees C) oven until lightly browned. Cool completely on wire rack.

Irish Oatmeal Cookies

Ingredients:

1 1/4 cups coconut oil
1/2 cup firmly packed brown sugar
1/2 cup white sugar
1 egg
1 tsp. vanilla extract
1 1/2 cups whole wheat flour
1 tsp. baking soda 1 tsp. coarse salt
3 cups quick-cooking Irish oatmeal
1 egg, beaten (optional)
1/2 cup golden raisins
1/2 cup chopped almonds

Directions:

1. Preheat oven to 350 degrees F (175 degrees C).
2. Grease 18 muffin cups with coconut oil.
3. Beat coconut oil, brown sugar, and white sugar with an electric mixer in a large bowl until smooth.
4. Mix in the flour mixture until just incorporated.
5. Beat 1 egg and vanilla extract into the coconut oil mixture.
6. Whisk flour, baking soda, and coarse salt together in a bowl.
7. Beat into the coconut oil mixture until a dough forms.
8. Fold oatmeal, raisins, and almonds into dough. Mix beaten egg into dough if needed for moisture.
9. Spoon dough into prepared muffin cups to about half full.
10. Bake in preheated oven until center is set and top is lightly browned, 12 to 14 minutes.

Highland Toffee

Ingredients:

1/3 cup vegetable oil
2 cups quick cooking oats
1/2 cup light brown sugar
1/4 cup light corn syrup
1/2 tsp. salt
1 1/2 tsps. vanilla extract
1 cup semisweet chocolate chips, melted
1/4 cup chopped nuts

Directions:

1. Preheat the oven to 400 degrees F (200 degrees C).
2. Generously grease an 8 or 9 inch square pan.
3. In a large bowl, stir together vegetable oil and oats.
4. Mix in brown sugar, corn syrup, salt, and vanilla.
5. Press mixture into prepared pan.
6. Bake for 12 minutes in preheated oven.
7. Set aside to cool.
8. Cut into 4 large squares to remove from pan.
9. Cover with melted chocolate, and sprinkle with nuts, if desired.
10. Allow the chocolate to cool, and then cut each square into 9 pieces.

Irish Peanut Butter Potato Candy

Ingredients:

1 potato, peeled and chopped
1 (32 oz.) package confectioners' sugar
1/4 cup creamy peanut butter, or as needed

Directions:

1. Place potato into a saucepan with enough water to cover and bring to a boil.
2. Reduce heat to medium-low and cook potato until very tender, about 15 minutes.
3. Drain and allow to steam dry for a minute or two.
4. Transfer potato to a large bowl and mash with a fork until smooth.
5. Gradually stir confectioners' sugar into mashed potato a little at a time until the mixture forms a stiff dough.
6. The dough will be runny until all the powdered sugar is used.
7. Place a large square of waxed paper onto a work surface.
8. Roll or press dough into a 12-inch square rectangle on the waxed paper.
9. Spread peanut butter over top of dough, covering it entirely.
10. Pick up one edge of waxed paper and start rolling the dough to make a 12-inch-long log. Wrap log tightly with waxed paper.
11. Refrigerate for 1 hour.
12. Unwrap log and slice candy into cross-sectional pieces about 3/4-inch thick to serve.

Irish Potatoes

Ingredients:

1 cup confectioners' sugar
1 cup shredded coconut
1 1/2 tbsps. cream
2 tbsps. ground cinnamon

Directions:

1. Sprinkle the sugar on the coconut.
2. Add the cream and mix gently.
3. Take approximately 1/2 tbsp. of dough and roll into balls.
4. Place cinnamon in a plastic bag and shake cookies a few at a time until coated.

Irish Cream Truffles

Ingredients:

1 cup heavy cream
1/4 cup white sugar
1/4 cup butter
1 (16 oz.) package semisweet chocolate chips
1 tbsp. Irish cream liqueur

Directions:

1. Whisk heavy cream and sugar together in a small saucepan over medium heat. Heat until the edges of the cream show fine bubbles but mixture does not boil, allowing sugar to dissolve.
2. Remove from heat.
3. Whisk butter, chocolate chips, and Irish cream into cream mixture until butter and chocolate chips are melted.
4. Cool to room temperature.
5. Scoop up the chocolate mixture about 1 tbsp. at a time and roll into a 1-inch ball.
6. Set truffles on a plate.
7. Refrigerate until firm, about 1 hour.

Bailey's Irish Cream Brownies

Ingredients:

2 (19.8 oz.) packages fudge brownie mix
1 cup Irish cream liqueur
2/3 cup vegetable oil
2 eggs
1 cup unsalted butter, softened
5 tbsps. Irish cream liqueur
4 cups confectioners' sugar

Directions:

1. Preheat oven to 350 degrees F (175 degrees C).
2. Butter the bottom of a 10 1/2x15 1/2-inch jelly roll pan.
3. Place fudge brownie mix into a large bowl.
4. Beat in 1 cup of Irish cream liqueur, vegetable oil, and eggs until the mixture forms a smooth batter.
5. Spread the batter into the prepared jelly roll pan.
6. Bake in the preheated oven until the brownies are set and a toothpick inserted into the center comes out clean, about 20 minutes.
7. Remove pan from oven and allow to cool completely.
8. Beat unsalted butter in a large bowl until smooth.
9. Beat in 5 tbsps.
10. Irish cream liqueur until mixture is creamy.
11. Slowly beat in confectioners' sugar, 1 cup at a time, until frosting is desired stiffness.
12. Spread frosting on brownies to serve.

Irish Cream Truffle Fudge

Ingredients:

3 cups semisweet chocolate chips
1 cup white chocolate chips
1/4 cup butter
3 cups confectioners' sugar
1 cup Irish cream liqueur
1 1/2 cups chopped nuts
1 cup semisweet chocolate chips
1/2 cup white chocolate chips
4 tbsps. Irish cream liqueur
2 tbsps. butter

Directions:

1. Butter a 8x8 inch pan.
2. In the top half of a double boiler melt the 3 cups semisweet chocolate chips, 1 cup white chocolate chips and 1/4 cup butter until soft enough to stir.
3. Stir in the confectioner's sugar and Irish cream until mixture is smooth. Stir in nuts.
4. Place mixture in the prepared pan and lay a sheet of plastic wrap over top; press and smooth top down.
5. In the top half of a double boiler melt remaining chocolates until soft. Remove from heat and with a fork beat in the butter and Irish cream until smooth. Spread topping over cooled fudge with a knife.
6. If a smooth top is important place plastic wrap over the top.
7. Refrigerate until firm, 1 to 2 hours at least.

Irish Cream Bundt Cake

Ingredients:

1 cup chopped pecans
1 (18.25 oz.) package yellow cake mix
1 (3.4 oz.) package instant vanilla pudding mix
4 eggs
1/4 cup water
1/2 cup vegetable oil
3/4 cup Irish cream liqueur
1/2 cup butter
1/4 cup water
1 cup white sugar
1/4 cup Irish cream liqueur

Directions:

1. Preheat oven to 325 degrees F (165 degrees C).
2. Grease and flour a 10 inch Bundt pan. Sprinkle chopped nuts evenly over bottom of pan.
3. In a large bowl, combine cake mix and pudding mix. Mix in eggs, 1/4 cup water, 1/2 cup oil and 3/4 cup Irish cream liqueur.
4. Beat for 5 minutes at high speed. Pour batter over nuts in pan.
5. Bake in the preheated oven for 60 minutes, or until a toothpick inserted into the cake comes out clean.
6. Cool for 10 minutes in the pan, then invert onto the serving dish.
7. Prick top and sides of cake. Spoon glaze over top and brush onto sides of cake. Allow to absorb glaze repeat until all glaze is used up.
8. To make the glaze: In a saucepan, combine butter, 1/4 cup water and 1 cup sugar.
9. Bring to a boil and continue boiling for 5 minutes, stirring constantly.
10. Remove from heat and stir in 1/4 cup Irish cream.

Irish Ginger Snaps

Ingredients:

1 cup white sugar
1 egg
1/4 tsp. salt
3/4 cup shortening
2 cups all-purpose flour
1/2 tsp. baking soda
1 tsp. ground cloves
1 tsp. ground ginger
1 tsp. ground cinnamon

Directions:

1. Preheat oven to 350 degrees F (175 degrees C).
2. Cream sugar, egg, salt and shortening together.
3. Add flour, baking soda and spices.
4. Mix well.
5. Roll teaspoonfuls of dough into balls and roll the balls in sugar.
6. Bake at 350 degrees F (175 degrees C) for 5 to 6 minutes.

Avocado Irish Cream Fudge

Ingredients:

2 avocados, peeled and pitted
1/2 cup butter, melted
1/2 cup Irish cream liqueur
2 cups unsweetened cocoa powder
6 cups confectioners' sugar
1 1/2 cups semisweet chocolate chips
1/2 cup white chocolate chips

Directions:

1. Place the avocados and melted butter in a mixing bowl.
2. Blend with an immersion blender until the mixture is smooth and creamy. Scrape the mixture into a saucepan and stir over low heat.
3. Pour in the Irish cream and stir.
4. Add the cocoa powder and stir until completely incorporated.
5. Stir in the confectioners' sugar 1 cup at a time, making sure the sugar is completely incorporated and the mixture is smooth before adding the next cup.
6. Melt the semi-sweet chocolate and white chocolate in a microwave-safe glass or ceramic bowl in 30-second intervals, stirring after each melting, for 1 to 3 minutes (depending on your microwave). Do not overheat or chocolate will scorch. Pour the melted chocolate into the sauce pan and mix thoroughly.
7. Remove from the heat.
8. Line a 9X11-inch pan with wax paper or foil sprayed with cooking spray. Pour the fudge mixture into the prepared pan.
9. Chill in the refrigerator for at least 1 hour.

Irish Cream Chocolate Cheesecake

Ingredients:

1 1/2 cups chocolate cookie crumbs
1/3 cup confectioners' sugar
1/3 cup unsweetened cocoa powder
1/4 cup butter
3 (8 oz.) packages cream cheese, softened
1 1/4 cups white sugar
1/4 cup unsweetened cocoa powder
3 tbsps. all-purpose flour
3 eggs
1/2 cup sour cream
1/4 cup Irish cream liqueur

Directions:

1. Preheat oven to 350 degrees F (175 degrees C).
2. In a large bowl, mix together the cookie crumbs, confectioners' sugar and 1/3 cup cocoa.
3. Add melted butter and stir until well mixed. Pat into the bottom of a 9 inch springform pan.
4. Bake in preheated oven for 10 minutes; set aside. Increase oven temperature to 450 degrees F (230 degrees C).
5. In a large bowl, combine cream cheese, white sugar, 1/4 cup cocoa and flour.
6. Beat at medium speed until well blended and smooth. Add eggs one at a time, mixing well after each addition. Blend in the sour cream and Irish cream liqueur; mixing on low speed. Pour filling over baked crust.
7. Bake at 450 degrees F (230 degrees C) for 10 minutes.
8. Reduce oven temperature to 250 degrees F (120 degrees C), and continue baking for 60 minutes.
9. With a knife, loosen cake from rim of pan. Let cool, then remove the rim of pan.
10. Chill before serving. If your cake cracks, a helpful tip is to dampen a spatula and smooth the top, then sprinkle with some chocolate wafer crumbs.

Irish Bannock

Ingredients:

2 cups all-purpose flour
2 tbsps. white sugar
1/2 tsp. baking powder
1/2 tsp. baking soda
1/2 tsp. salt
2 tbsps. butter
1 cup buttermilk
1/2 cup dried currants

Directions:

1. Combine flour, sugar, baking soda, baking powder, and salt.
2. Cut butter into flour mixture with pastry cutter.
3. Add buttermilk until dough is soft.
4. Stir in currants.
5. Turn dough out onto a lightly floured surface.
6. Knead for 5 minutes, or until smooth.
7. Form dough into a 7 inch round.
8. Place on a lightly oiled cake pan or cookie sheet.
9. Cut 1/2 inch deep cross side to side. Score with cross 1/2 inch deep on the top.
10. Bake in a preheated 375 degrees F (190 degrees C) oven for 40 minutes.

Irish Bananas

Ingredients:

1/2 cup butter
1/2 cup packed light brown sugar
1/2 cup Irish whiskey
4 large bananas, peeled and halved lengthwise

Directions:

1. Melt the butter in a skillet over medium heat.
2. Stir in the brown sugar and whiskey.
3. Bring to a boil and cook until sugar has dissolved.
4. Add bananas to the skillet and simmer gently until bananas are tender and glazed with the syrup.
5. Serve immediately with vanilla ice cream.

Irish Barmbrack

This cake is traditionally eaten around Halloween but is still great to have when celebrating St. Patrick's Day.

Ingredients:

2 1/2 cups chopped dried mixed fruit
1 1/2 cups hot brewed tea
2 1/2 cups flour
1 tsp. ground cinnamon
1/2 tsp. ground nutmeg
1/2 tsp. baking soda
1 egg
1 1/2 cups sugar
1/4 cup lemon marmalade
1 tsp. grated orange zest

Directions:

1. Soak the dried fruit in the hot tea for 2 hours, then drain and gently squeeze out excess tea.
2. Preheat oven to 350 degrees F (175 degrees C).
3. Grease a 9 inch Bundt pan.
4. Stir together the flour cinnamon, nutmeg, and baking soda; set aside.
5. Beat the egg, sugar, marmalade, orange zest, and tea-soaked fruit until well combined.
6. Gently fold in the flour until just combined, then pour into the prepared Bundt pan.
7. Bake in preheated oven for 1 hour or until the top of the cake springs back when lightly pressed.
8. Allow to cool in the pan for 2 hours before removing.
9. Continue to cool to room temperature on a wire rack.
10. Press the objects of choice into the cake through the bottom before serving.

Irish Apple Pie

Ingredients:

1 1/2 cups all-purpose flour
3/4 cup cake flour
1/2 tsp. salt
1 tbsp. white sugar
1 cup unsalted butter
3 tbsps. shortening
1/4 cup sour cream
1/8 tsp. lemon juice
5 large Granny Smith apples, peeled, cored and sliced
1/2 cup white sugar
2 tbsps. all-purpose flour
1/2 tbsp. ground nutmeg
1/8 tsp. lemon juice
1 egg, beaten

Directions:

1. Preheat oven to 350 degrees F (175 degrees C).
2. Grease a 9 inch pie pan.
3. In a large bowl, combine flours, salt and sugar.
4. Cut in butter and shortening until coarse crumbs are formed. Mix in sour cream and lemon juice. Keep mixing until dough forms a ball; dough may be slightly lumpy, this is fine. Wrap dough ball in plastic wrap and allow to chill for 1 hour.
5. Once chilled, take dough out of refrigerator and cut it in half.
6. Keep one half covered and in the refrigerator. Roll dough to 1/8 of an inch. To lift pie shell, roll dough around rolling pin and then unroll into pie pan. Trim overhanging edges of pie crust.
7. Place apples into pie shell. In a small bowl, combine sugar, flour and nutmeg; mix thoroughly. Sprinkle mixture over apples.
8. Squirt lemon juice over apples.
9. Place pie in refrigerator while top crust is rolled out.
10. Remove pie from refrigerator.
11. Brush outer edge of bottom crust with beaten egg. Place second crust on top of pie; crimp pie shell edges together. Brush entire top crust with egg and cut 4 steam slots into it.
12. Bake in a preheated 350 degrees F (175 degrees C) oven for 45 minutes, or until golden brown.

13. Allow pie to completely cool before serving. Serve warm with whipped cream or vanilla ice cream.

Irish Beef and Guinness Pies

Ingredients:

1 1/2 lb. beef chuck or stew meat trimmed and cut into 1" pieces
5 tbsp. flour
Kosher salt
Black pepper
3 tbsp. olive oil
6 shallots, chopped
4 large portobello mushrooms (about 14 oz.), cut into 1" pieces
2 large carrots, cut into 1/4" pieces
2 cloves garlic, smashed
1 celery stalk, finely chopped
1 Sprig Fresh Thyme
1 (14.9 oz.) can Guinness
4 cup low-sodium beef broth
1 1/2 tbsp. unsalted butter
1 oz. bittersweet chocolate, finely chopped
2 sheets frozen puff pastry from a 17.3 oz. package), thawed
1 large egg, beaten

Directions:

1. In a large bowl, toss the beef with 2 tbsps. flour and 1/2 tsp. each salt and pepper. Heat 1 tbsp. oil in a large pot or Dutch oven over medium heat. In two batches, brown the beef on all sides, about 5 minutes total (add 1 tbsp. oil for the second batch); transfer to a plate.
2. Add the remaining 1 tbsp. oil to the pot. Add the shallots, mushrooms, carrots, garlic, celery and thyme and cook, stirring occasionally, until beginning to soften, about 5 minutes.
3. Return the beef to the pot with the Guinness and beef broth (make sure beef and vegetables are covered completely, adding additional water if necessary). Simmer gently, stirring occasionally, until beef is tender, 1 1/2 to 2 hours.
4. Once the beef is done, strain the cooking liquid into a large measuring cup (you should still have 3 to 4 cups).
5. Return the beef and vegetables to the pot, discarding the thyme. Melt the butter with 1/2 cup cooking liquid in a medium saucepan over medium heat. Stir in the remaining 3 tbsps. flour to form a smooth paste.
6. Gradually whisk in the rest of the strained cooking liquid and simmer until slightly thickened, 4 to 5 minutes. Add the chocolate and stir to melt. Pour the sauce over the beef and vegetables and let cool.

7. Arrange one rack on the bottom of the oven and heat to 350 degrees F. Working with one sheet at a time, on a lightly floured surface, roll out the pastry into a 14" square and cut out two 8" circles and two 6" circles.
8. Fit the 8" cutouts into the bottom and up the sides of two 6" pie plates.
9. Repeat with the remaining sheet.
10. Divide the beef mixture among the pie plates (about 1 1/2 cups per plate). use the 6" cutouts to cover each pie, pinching the edges to seal.
11. Lightly brush the pastry with the egg, then use a sharp knife to cut 2 diagonal slits in the top of each piece of pastry. Place the pies on a rimmed baking sheet and bake on the lowest rack until the pastry is puffed and golden brown, 45 minutes.

Lucky Charms Cookies

Ingredients:

2 cups Lucky Charms (just cereal, no marshmallows)
1½ cups all-purpose flour
1 tsp. baking soda
1 tsp. salt
2 stick butter
1 cup granulated sugar
¾ cup packed light brown sugar
2 large eggs
1 cup Lucky Charms marshmallow bits
½ cup white chocolate chips

Directions:

1. Line a large jelly-roll pan with parchment paper.
2. In food processor, pulse Lucky Charms 1 minute or until finely ground; transfer cereal to large bowl. Add flour, baking soda, and salt and whisk until combined.
3. In large bowl, with a mixer on medium speed, beat butter, granulated sugar, and brown sugar for 4 minutes, or until light and fluffy. Beat in the eggs, 1 at a time, until combined.
4. Reduce mixer speed to medium-low.
5. Add flour mixture all at once and beat until it is just combined.
6. Fold in marshmallow bits and chocolate chips using a spatula or wooden spoon.
7. Cover and refrigerate dough 30 minutes.
8. Preheat the oven to 375 degrees F. Scoop rounded tablespoonfuls of dough onto prepared cookie sheet, about 2 inches apart. Bake 8 to 10 minutes or until pale golden. Let the cookies cool on the pan for 5 minutes, then transfer them to wire racks to cool completely.

Lucky Charms Eclairs

Ingredients:

1 c. Lucky Charms
1 c. all-purpose flour
1 c. water
8 tbsp. butter
½ tsp. salt
4 large eggs
2 bar white chocolate
½ c. heavy cream
green food coloring
⅓ c. store-bought lemon or lime curd
1 c. Sweetened whipped cream
Lucky Charm marshmallow bits

Directions:

1. Preheat the oven to 400 degrees F. Line a large jelly-roll pan with parchment paper.
2. In a food processor, pulse the Lucky Charms for 1 minute or until they are finely ground; transfer the cereal to a medium bowl, add flour, and whisk until combined.
3. In 3-quart saucepan, heat water, butter, and salt to boiling on medium until butter melts. Vigorously stir in flour mixture all at once until mixture forms ball and comes away from side of pan, about 3 minutes. Remove from heat; let cool slightly.
4. Add the eggs, 1 at a time, beating well after each addition, until the batter becomes smooth and satiny.
5. Transfer the batter to a pastry bag fitted with a large round tip (or a plastic bag with the corner snipped off).
6. On the prepared pan, pipe 4- to 5-inch long strips of dough; flatten any points with a damp fingertip. Bake 35 to 40 minutes, or until golden brown.
7. Turn off the oven; keep éclairs in the oven while it cools, 15 minutes more. Transfer to wire rack to cool.
8. Put the white chocolate into a medium heatproof bowl. In small saucepan on medium, bring heavy cream to boiling. Pour over chocolate; let sit 5 minutes. Whisk until melted and smooth. Tint with green food coloring, if desired.

9. In another medium bowl, fold together the lemon curd and whipped cream until smooth. Transfer to resealable plastic bag; snip small piece from corner.
10. For each éclair, stick skewer in one end of pastry and twirl around to hollow out inside. Insert plastic bag corner into hole and squeeze in filling. Top with glaze using offset spatula. Top with marshmallow bits, if desired.

Irish Earl Grey Tea Cookies

Ingredients:

2 3/4 cup all-purpose flour
2 tbsp. fine Earl Grey tea leaves
1/2 tsp. baking powder
1/4 tsp. kosher salt
1 cup unsalted butter
¾ cup granulated sugar
1 large egg
1 tsp. grated orange zest

Directions:

1. In a large bowl, whisk together the flour, tea leaves, baking powder, and salt.
2. In a food processor, process the butter and sugar until smooth.
3. Add the egg and orange zest and pulse to combine. Add the flour mixture and pulse to combine.
4. Transfer the mixture to a lightly floured surface and roll into two logs, about 2 inch in diameter.
5. Wrap each in plastic wrap, tightly twisting the ends, and chill for at least 30 minutes.
6. Heat the oven to 350 degrees F.
7. Line large baking sheets with parchment paper.
8. Slice the cookies 1/8 inch thick and place on the prepared baking sheet, spacing them 1 inch apart.
9. Bake, rotating the sheets halfway through, until the cookies are lightly golden brown around the edges, 14 to 16 minutes. Let cool for 5 minutes on the baking sheets, then transfer to a wire rack to cool completely.

Irish Thin-Mint Grasshopper Pie

Ingredients:

1 box dark-chocolate thin mints
1 1/4 cup heavy (whipping) cream
1 ready-to-fill chocolate crumb crust
25 large marshmallows
1/4 cup each white crème de cacao and green crème de menthe
Garnish: whipped cream, thin mints and mint sprigs

Directions:

1. Reserve 4 thin mints for garnish.
2. Put remaining 26 mints in a small saucepan; add 2 Tbsp. cream.
3. Stir over medium-low heat 1 to 2 minutes until melted and smooth. (Or microwave in a 4-cup glass measure about 1 minute.)
4. Pour into crumb crust and place in freezer to cool until firm, about 30 minutes.
5. Meanwhile, put marshmallows and crème de cacao in a medium saucepan over medium-low heat.
6. Stir with a whisk 4 to 5 minutes until melted and smooth.
7. Whisk in crème de menthe; place in freezer to cool about 10 minutes.
8. Put remaining cream in a large, deep bowl.
9. Beat with mixer until stiff peaks form when beaters are lifted.
10. Whisk cooled liqueur mixture to recombine, then fold into the cream until well blended. Pour over thin-mint layer.
11. Cover and freeze at least 24 hours.
12. Garnish before serving.
13. To make clean cuts, use a long, sharp knife, and dip in hot water between cuts.

Fried Irish Cabbage with Bacon

Ingredients:

1 (12 oz.) package bacon
1/4 cup bacon drippings
1 small head cabbage, cored and chopped
Ground black pepper to taste

Directions:

1. Cook bacon in a deep skillet over medium heat until crisp, 5 to 7 minutes.
2. Remove bacon from skillet and drain on a paper towel-lined plate. Reserve 1/4 cup drippings in skillet.
3. Cook and stir cabbage in hot bacon drippings over medium heat until cabbage wilts, 5 to 7 minutes.
4. Crumble bacon over cabbage.
5. Stir and simmer until bacon is warmed, 2 to 3 minutes.
6. Season with black pepper.

Irish Lucky Charms Cheesecakes

Crust Ingredients:
3 cup Lucky Charms (just cereal, no marshmallows)
6 tbsp. butter
Filling
½ cup heavy cream
1 cup Lucky Charms (cereal and marshmallow bits)
2 package cream cheese
1 cup granulated sugar
1 tsp. vanilla extract
.13 tsp. salt
3 large eggs
Green food coloring
Topping Ingredients:
½ cup wweetened whipped cream
Lucky Charm marshmallow bits

Directions:

1. Make the crust: Preheat the oven to 350 degrees F.
2. Line miniature muffin pans with liners.
3. In food processor, pulse the Lucky Charms for 1 minute, or until finely ground.
4. Add butter; pulse until the mixture resembles wet sand.
5. Press 1 heaping tsp. of the crumb mixture into the bottom of each liner. Bake 5 minutes or until lightly golden.
6. Cool completely.
7. In small saucepan on medium, bring heavy cream and cereal to boiling.
8. Remove from heat; set aside 15 minutes.
9. Strain through fine-mesh sieve into liquid measuring cup, pressing down on solids with spatula to release any liquid.
10. In large bowl, with mixer on medium speed, beat cream cheese and sugar 3 minutes or until fluffy. Beat in vanilla and salt until combined. Add eggs, 1 at a time, beating well after each addition.
11. Beat in heavy cream. Tint with green food coloring, if desired.
12. Divide filling among prepared liners. Bake 12 to 13 minutes or until set but still slightly wiggly and moist in centers. Let cool in pans 5 minutes, then transfer to wire racks to cool completely.
13. Refrigerate at least 30 minutes. Top each with 1 dollop whipped cream and 1 marshmallow bit, if desired.

Irish Blueberry Scones

Ingredients:

1 3/4 cup all purpose flour
2 tbsps. sugar
1 tbsp. baking powder
1/4 tsp. salt
4 tbsps. unsalted butter, sliced into pats
1/2 cup dried blueberries
5 tbsps. milk
1 egg, plus 1 more beaten to brush on top

Directions:

1. Heat the oven to 375F. Line a baking sheet with parchment paper.
2. Whisk the flour, sugar, baking powder and salt together in a large bowl. Rub in the butter with your fingers until it's all worked in.
3. Mix in the blueberries.
4. In a small bowl or measuring cup, whisk the milk and one egg together.
5. Pour the milk mixture in with the dry ingredients and gently mix until the liquid is fully incorporated.
6. Transfer the dough to a lightly floured surface.
7. Knead the dough a few times and pat it into a disc about ¾" thick.
8. Divide the dough into 8 equal wedges -- transfer the wedges to the prepared baking sheet, leaving space between each scone.
9. Bake the scones for 15-20 minutes, until the tops are lightly browned. Serve warm with butter!

Irish Lemon Pudding

Ingredients:

2 tbsps. butter
1/4 cup sugar
2 eggs, separated
1/2 cup flour
2 lemons, zested and juiced
1 1/4 cups milk

Directions:

1. Preheat oven to 350. Cream the butter and sugar well.
2. Add the egg yolks one by one, then add the flour.
3. Add the lemon zest and juice, followed by the milk, and mix well.
4. In a separate bowl, whisk the egg whites until stiff.
5. Fold gently into the lemon mixture until incorporated.
6. Pour into a 8-9 inch pie pan or cake pan.
7. Bake for 40 minutes, or until very lightly browned and set.
8. Sprinkle with powdered sugar and serve warm with freshly whipped cream.

Irish Beef Beer Stew

Ingredients:

2 tbsps. olive oil
1 onion, chopped
3 cloves garlic, minced
1 tsp. salt
1/2 tsp. ground black pepper
2 pounds beef stew meat, cubed
3 cups stout beer (such as Guinness®)
2 potatoes, peeled and sliced
2 potatoes, peeled and quartered
Salt and ground black pepper to taste

Directions:

1. Heat the olive oil in a large pot over medium heat.
2. Stir in the onion, garlic, salt, and pepper.
3. Cook and stir until the onion has softened and turned translucent, about 5 minutes.
4. Stir in the beef, beer, sliced potatoes, and quartered potatoes.
5. Bring to a boil over high heat, then reduce heat to medium-low, cover, and simmer until the beef is tender, about 2 hours.
6. Season to taste with salt and pepper before serving.

Irish Tea Cake

Ingredients:

1/2 cup butter, softened
1 cup white sugar
2 eggs
1 1/2 tsps. vanilla extract
1 3/4 cups all-purpose flour
2 tsps. baking powder
1/2 tsp. salt
1/2 cup milk
1/4 cup confectioners' sugar for dusting

Directions:

1. Preheat oven to 350 degrees F (175 degrees C).
2. Grease and flour a 9-inch round pan.
3. In a medium bowl, cream together the butter and sugar until light and fluffy.
4. Beat in the eggs, one at a time, mixing until fully incorporated.
5. Stir in the vanilla.
6. Combine the flour, baking powder and salt; stir into the batter alternately with the milk. If the batter is too stiff, a tbsp. or two of milk may be added.
7. Spread the batter evenly into the prepared pan.
8. Bake for 30 to 35 minutes in the preheated oven, until a toothpick inserted into the center comes out clean.
9. Cool in pan on a wire rack, then turn out onto a serving plate.
10. Dust with confectioners' sugar right before serving.

Irish Whiskey and Beer Cupcakes

Ingredients:

1 cup Irish stout beer (such as Guinness®)
1 cup butter
3/4 cup unsweetened cocoa powder
2 cups all-purpose flour
2 cups white sugar
1 1/2 tsps. baking soda
3/4 tsp. salt
2 large eggs
2/3 cup sour cream
2/3 cup heavy whipping cream
8 oz. bittersweet chocolate, chopped
2 tbsps. butter
1 tsp. Irish whiskey, or more to taste
1/2 cup butter, softened
3 cups confectioners' sugar, or more as needed
3 tbsps. Irish cream liqueur (such as Baileys®), or more to taste

Directions:

1. Preheat oven to 350 degrees F (175 degrees C).
2. Line 24 muffin cups with paper liners.
3. Bring Irish stout beer and 1 cup butter to a boil in a saucepan and set aside until butter has melted, stirring occasionally.
4. Mix in cocoa powder until smooth.
5. Whisk together flour, sugar, baking soda, and salt in a bowl until thoroughly combined.
6. Beat eggs with sour cream in a large bowl with an electric mixer on low until well combined. Slowly beat in the beer mixture, then the flour mixture; beat until the batter is smooth.
7. Divide batter between the prepared cupcake cups, filling each cup about 2/3 full.
8. Bake in the preheated oven until a toothpick inserted into the center of a cupcake comes out clean, about 17 minutes.
9. Cool the cupcakes completely.
10. Cut cores out of the center of each cupcake with a sharp paring knife. Discard cores.
11. Bring cream to a simmer in a saucepan over low heat; stir in bittersweet chocolate until melted.

12. Mix in 2 tbsps. butter and Irish whiskey until butter is melted; let mixture cool to room temperature.
13. Filling will thicken as it cools.
14. Spoon the filling into the cored cupcakes.
15. For frosting, whip 1/2 cup butter in a bowl with an electric mixer until fluffy, 2 to 3 minutes.
16. Set mixer to low speed and slowly beat in confectioners' sugar, 1 cup at a time, until frosting is smooth and spreadable. Beat in the Irish cream liqueur; adjust thickness of frosting with more confectioners' sugar if needed.
17. Spread frosting on filled cupcakes.

Irish Stout and Chocolate Cheesecake

Ingredients:

1 cup crushed chocolate cookies
1/4 cup butter, softened
2 tbsps. white sugar
1/4 tsp. unsweetened cocoa powder
3 (8 oz.) packages cream cheese, softened
1 cup white sugar
3 eggs
1/2 pound semisweet chocolate chips
2 tbsps. heavy cream
1 cup sour cream
1 pinch salt
3/4 cup Irish stout beer (e.g. Guinness®)
2 tsps. vanilla extract
1 (1 oz.) square semisweet chocolate

Directions:

1. Preheat oven to 350 degrees F (175 degrees C).
2. Prepare a 9 inch spring form pan with butter.
3. Combine the crushed cookies, butter, 2 tbsps. sugar, and cocoa in a small bowl; mix; press into the bottom of the prepared spring form pan.
4. Place the cream cheese in a large bowl and beat with an electric mixer set to low speed until smooth.
5. While beating, slowly add 1 cup sugar and then the eggs, one at a time. Continue beating until smooth.
6. Combine the chocolate chips and heavy cream in a microwave-safe bowl.
7. Heat in the microwave until the chocolate is completely melted, stirring every 30 seconds.
8. Beat the chocolate into the cream cheese mixture.
9. Add the sour cream, salt, beer, and vanilla; blend until smooth.
10. Pour the mixture over the crust.
11. Place the pan into a large, deep baking dish.
12. Fill the dish with water to cover the bottom half of the spring form pan.
13. Bake the cheesecake in the water bath in the preheated oven for 45 minutes; turn oven off; leave the cheesecake in the oven with oven door slightly ajar another 45 minutes; remove from oven.
14. Run a knife along the edge of the cheesecake to loosen from pan.

15. Chill in refrigerator at least 4 hours.
16. Melt the semisweet chocolate in a small bowl using the microwave.
17. Make chocolate clovers by dropping 3 small drops of melted chocolate close to one another on waxed paper. Drag a toothpick from between two dots outward to make the stem; chill until hardened.
18. Arrange the chocolate clovers on top of the chilled cheesecake for decoration.

Irish Cheese Soup

Ingredients:

5 cups vegetable stock
5 cups Irish-style lager
Salt and ground black pepper to taste
2 1/2 pounds Yukon Gold potatoes, peeled and diced
5 cups heavy cream
3/4 leek, sliced
1/2 tsp. minced garlic
1 sprig fresh thyme, chopped
1 pinch cayenne pepper, or to taste
5 cups shredded Irish Cheddar cheese (such as Dubliner®)

Directions:

1. Combine vegetable stock and lager in a stock pot; season with salt and black pepper; bring to a simmer over medium-low heat.
2. Cook potatoes in the simmering stock mixture until tender, 20 to 30 minutes.
3. Stir cream, leek, garlic, and thyme into the stock mixture; bring to a boil, return heat to medium-low, and cook at a simmer another 10 minutes.
4. Sprinkle cayenne pepper into the soup.
5. Melt cheese into the soup 1 cup at a time while blending with an immersion blender until smooth.

Bangers and Mash

Ingredients:

4 links pork sausage
2 pounds potatoes, peeled and cubed
1/4 cup butter
2 tbsps. milk (optional)
1 tsp. dry mustard powder
Salt and ground black pepper to taste
1 tbsp. butter
2 large onions, chopped
6 cups beef broth
2 cups red wine

Directions:

1. Preheat oven to 200 degrees F (95 degrees C).
2. Cook the sausage links in a skillet over medium-low heat until browned on all sides, about 5 minutes per side; transfer to an oven-safe dish and move to the preheated oven to keep warm.
3. Place potatoes into a saucepan over medium heat, cover with water, and boil gently until potatoes are tender, 10 to 15 minutes.
4. Drain and allow to steam dry for a minute or two. Mix in 1/4 cup of butter, milk, dry mustard, salt, and black pepper; mash until fluffy and smooth. Set aside.
5. Melt 1 tbsp. butter in a skillet over medium-high heat; cook the onions until translucent and just starting to brown, about 8 minutes.
6. Pour in the beef broth and red wine; boil the mixture down to about half its volume, about 10 minutes. Season with salt and black pepper.
7. To serve, place a sausage onto a serving plate with about 1/2 cup of mashed potatoes.
8. Pour the onion gravy over the sausage and potatoes.

Irish Cheese Dip

Ingredients:

1 1/2 cups shredded Irish Cheddar cheese (such as Dubliner®)
1 cup plain yogurt
1/2 cup finely chopped green onions
1/4 cup mayonnaise
2 tsps. prepared horseradish
1 tsp. ground black pepper

Directions:

1. Stir Cheddar cheese, yogurt, green onions, mayonnaise, horseradish, and black pepper together in a bowl.
2. Refrigerate until chilled, at least 1 hour.

Irish Toast

Ingredients:

1 (16 oz.) loaf French bread
4 large eggs
1 fluid oz. Irish whiskey
1 1/2 fluid oz. Irish cream liqueur
1 tsp. vanilla extract
1/4 cup butter
Confectioners' sugar for dusting

Directions:

1. Cut the bread into 12 slices. In a bowl, whisk together the eggs, Irish whiskey, Irish cream liqueur, and vanilla extract until well blended.
2. Heat some of the butter in a skillet over medium heat until the butter is hot and the foam has disappeared.
3. Press each bread slice into the egg mixture, then fry in the hot skillet until nicely browned on both sides, about 2 minutes per side.
4. Add more butter to skillet as needed.
5. Brush each slice with butter, and sprinkle with confectioners' sugar.

Irish Brown Bread

Ingredients:

1 cup all-purpose flour
2 tbsps. white sugar
1 tsp. baking powder
1 tsp. baking soda
1/2 tsp. salt
1 1/2 tbsps. butter
2 cups whole wheat flour
1/4 cup quick-cooking oatmeal
1 1/2 cups nonfat plain yogurt
1 tsp. milk, or more as needed (optional)

Directions:

1. Preheat the oven to 375 degrees F (190 degrees C).
2. Lightly grease a baking sheet.
3. Mix all-purpose flour, sugar, baking powder, baking soda, and salt in a bowl.
4. Cut butter into flour mixture with a pastry blender or 2 knives until the mixture forms fine crumbs.
5. Stir whole-wheat flour and quick-cooking oatmeal into the butter mixture.
6. Gently stir yogurt into the oatmeal mixture. If mixture is too dry to hold together, add 1 tsp. milk at a time, just until dough holds together; it should not be sticky.
7. Turn the dough out onto a lightly floured work surface; knead gently about 5 times to form a ball.
8. Place the dough in the center of the prepared baking sheet; cut a large 'X' in the top of the loaf.
9. Bake in preheated oven until well browned, about 40 minutes; transfer to a rack to cool. Bread can be served warm or cold.

Irish Stuffed Baked Potato

Ingredients:

2 large baking potatoes
1 1/2 cups finely chopped cabbage
1/2 cup finely chopped onion
4 slices bacon, chopped
1/2 cup milk 1/4 cup butter
1/4 tsp. ground black pepper salt to taste
3/4 cup shredded Cheddar cheese, divided

Directions:

1. Preheat oven to 350 degrees F (175 degrees C).
2. Scrub potatoes, pierce several times with a fork, and place on microwave-safe plate.
3. Cook potatoes on High in microwave 5 minutes; turn over and cook until soft, about 5 minutes more. Scoop potato flesh into a bowl; reserve potato skins.
4. Cook and stir cabbage, onion, and bacon in a skillet over medium heat until vegetables are soft, about 10 minutes.
5. Stir milk, butter, pepper, and salt into cabbage mixture; stir in potato flesh and 1/2 cup of Cheddar cheese.
6. Cook and stir cabbage mixture, breaking up potato and mashing lightly, until milk is absorbed, about 5 minutes.
7. Remove pan from heat; pile potato mixture into potato skins and place stuffed potatoes in a baking dish. Sprinkle potatoes with remaining Cheddar cheese.
8. Bake in the preheated oven until cheese is bubbly and potatoes are heated through, about 25 minutes.

About the Author

Laura Sommers is **The Recipe Lady!**

She is the #1 Best Selling Author of over 80 recipe books.

She is a loving wife and mother who lives on a small farm in Baltimore County, Maryland and has a passion for all things domestic especially when it comes to saving money. She has a profitable eBay business and is a couponing addict, avid blogger and YouTuber.

Follow her tips and tricks to learn how to make delicious meals on a budget, save money or to learn the latest life hack!

Visit my blog for even more great recipes and to learn which books are **FREE** for download each week:

http://the-recipe-lady.blogspot.com/

Visit her Amazon Author Page to see her latest books:

amazon.com/author/laurasommers

Other books in This Series

- Super Awesome Traditional Maryland Recipes

- Super Awesome Traditional Philadelphia Recipes

- Authentic Traditional Pennsylvania Dutch Amish and Mennonite Recipes

- Authentic Traditional Memphis, Tennessee Recipes

- Traditional Vermont Recipes

- Traditional Kentucky Recipes

- Oktoberfest Recipes for the German Beer Festival

- Best Traditional Cajun and Creole Recipes from New Orleans

May all of your meals be a banquet
with good friends and good food.

Printed in Great Britain
by Amazon